Sugarcraf

MODELLI